BOOK FOUR

WILLARD A. PALMER AND AMANDA VICK LETHCO

CREATING MUSIC
at the piano

D1303785

This book belongs to _____

The Sloop John B.

Sea Chanty

3

TRIADS IN ALL POSITIONS

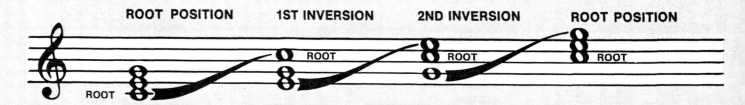

ROOT POSITION   1ST INVERSION   2ND INVERSION   ROOT POSITION

PLAY THE FOLLOWING:

Drop on the 1st count. Hold on the 2nd count.

Lift on the rest, to prepare to drop on the next triad.

Play with the R.H. as written.

Then play with the L.H., an octave lower.

1. KEY OF C MAJOR

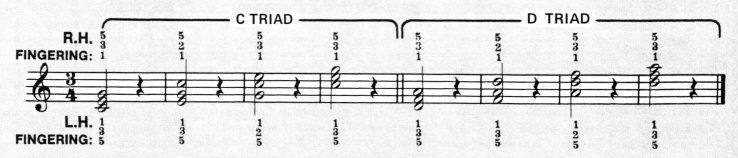

(Continue up the scale, beginning on the **E** triad, the **F** triad, the **G** triad, etc.)

2. KEY OF G MAJOR

(Continue up the scale, beginning on the **B** triad, the **C** triad, etc.
Carefully observe the key signature.)

3. KEY OF D MAJOR

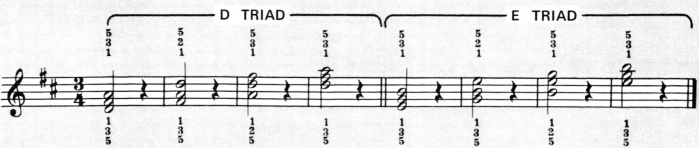

(Continue up the scale, beginning on the **F#** triad, the **G** triad, etc.
Carefully observe the key signature.)

America

Adagio e maestoso (*Slowly and majestically*)

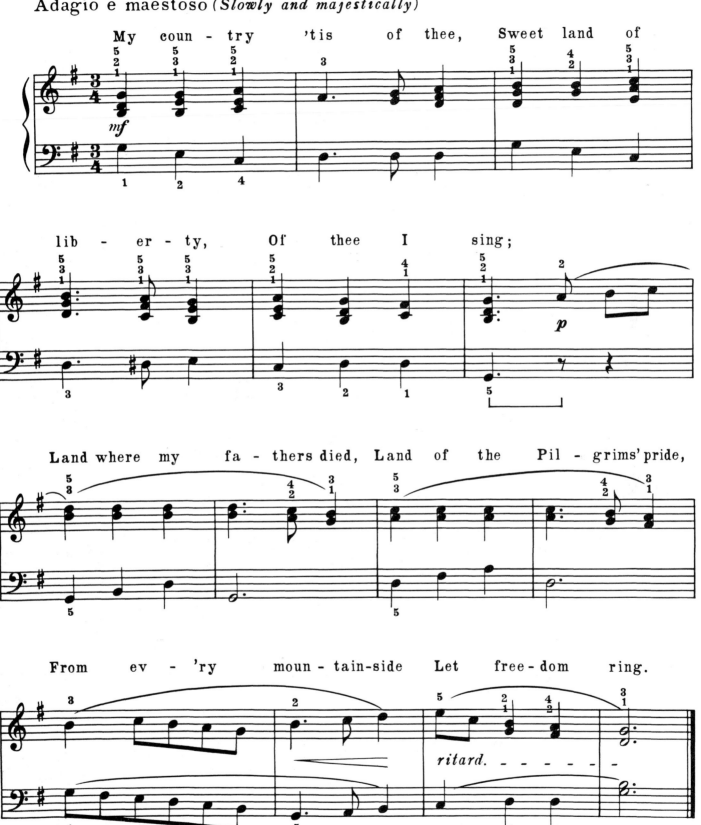

CIRCLE THE ROOT OF EACH R.H. TRIAD IN THE FIRST TWO LINES OF "AMERICA."

THE **F** MAJOR SCALE

KEY-NOTE

| 1st TETRACHORD | WHOLE STEP | 2nd TETRACHORD |

REMEMBER! THE PATTERN OF EACH TETRACHORD IS:
WHOLE STEP—WHOLE STEP—HALF STEP

PLAY:

p -f

R. H. 2   5

L. H. 5   L. H. 2

RIGHT HAND:

To play the **F** Major Scale with the R.H., the thumb must cross under the 4th finger.

REMEMBER: Lift the wrist slightly and lean the hand in the direction
you are going. Drop the thumb on the outside tip.

legato
p-f

LEFT HAND:

To play the **F** Major Scale with the L.H., the thumb crosses under **3** as usual.

legato
p-f

Country Gardens

Brightly

Old English Dance

KEY of F MAJOR
Key signature: ONE FLAT (B♭)

PLAN FOR A TUNE IN **F** MAJOR

With this plan you can make tunes in the KEY OF **F** MAJOR.

Play the plan.

Use the THUMB on each R.H. note.

Practice the plan until you can play it with ease!

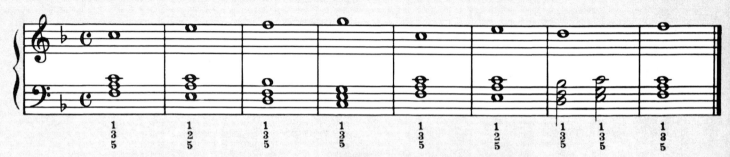

Make a tune from the following motive, using the steps outlined below:

MOTIVE No. 1:

STEP A: Play the motive with the R.H., using the 1st treble note
of the plan **(C)** as the starting note of the motive.
Proceed to the next measure,
and use the next treble note **(E)** as the starting note.
Continue, using the motive in each measure except the last.
BE SURE TO OBSERVE THE KEY SIGNATURE. ALL **B's** ARE FLAT.

STEP B: Add the BASS. The L.H. plays only the notes shown in the plan.
Choose your own tempo and dynamics!

MOTIVE No. 1
in the plan

etc.

MAKE A TUNE FROM EACH OF THE FOLLOWING MOTIVES.
Use STEPS A and B, above.

MOTIVE No. 2.   **MOTIVE No. 3.**

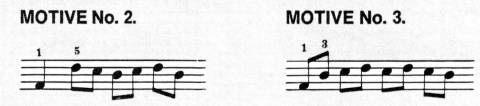

CREATE A MOTIVE OF YOUR OWN AND USE IT IN THE PLAN.

Laredo

This favorite Mexican folk song was used by the great American composer, Aaron Copland, as one of the themes in his famous symphonic composition, *El Salon Mexico.* Practice R.H. alone until you can play it with ease, then add the **OSTINATO** (repeating) **BASS.**

Andante moderato

Traditional

---

*IMPORTANT!
POCO is an Italian word meaning "little."   *poco ritardando* = slowing a little.

REPEATED NOTE WARM-UPS

MASTER THESE TWO WARM-UPS THOROUGHLY
BEFORE PROCEEDING TO "COMEDIANS' DANCE."

PRACTICE VERY SLOWLY AT FIRST.
AS EACH WARM-UP IS MASTERED, IT MAY BE PLAYED FASTER.

DROP THE 3rd FINGER ON THE FIRST NOTE OF EACH GROUP OF THREE.

Comedians' Dance

Dmitri Kabalevsky was born in St. Petersburg, Russia, in 1904. He has composed choral music, symphonic music, ballet music and opera. His piano works are especially famous and are characterized by their energetic rhythms and good humor.

Allegro KEY of F MAJOR

Kabalevsky

* 8va segue: An octave higher, CONTINUING (in this case, through the entire piece).

Fine

D. C. al Fine

INTRODUCING MINOR KEYS

The modern system of keys and key signatures developed from the ancient modes.

The IONIAN mode became the key of **C MAJOR.**
The AEOLIAN mode became the key of **A MINOR.**

Because the keys of **C MAJOR** and **A MINOR** have the same key signature, they are called RELATIVES.

The RELATIVE MINOR scale begins on the 6th TONE of the MAJOR SCALE.

C MAJOR SCALE

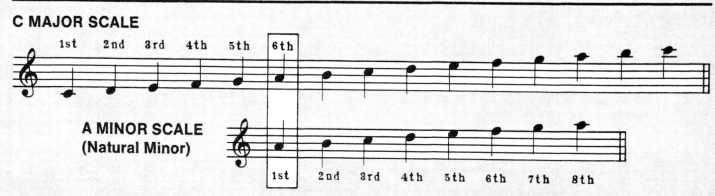

The 6th TONE of the MAJOR SCALE becomes the 1st TONE of the RELATIVE MINOR.

LEARN: A MINOR IS THE RELATIVE MINOR OF C MAJOR.

F MAJOR SCALE

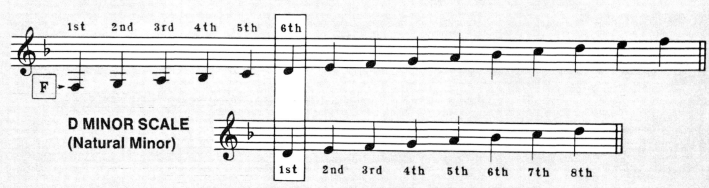

LEARN: D MINOR IS THE RELATIVE MINOR OF F MAJOR.

WRITE THE RELATIVE MINOR OF G MAJOR ON THE 2nd STAFF BELOW:

G MAJOR SCALE

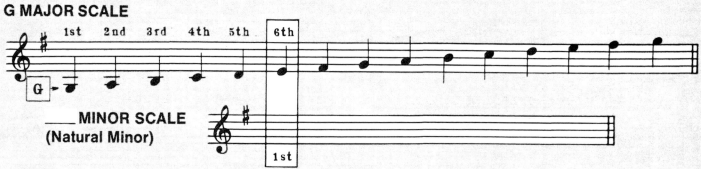

FILL IN: ____ MINOR IS THE RELATIVE MINOR OF G MAJOR.

THE A MINOR SCALES IN CONTRARY MOTION

Practice each scale on this page with hands separately, then with hands together.
THERE ARE 3 IMPORTANT FORMS OF THE MINOR SCALE:

1. The NATURAL or PURE Minor Scale.

This scale uses EXACTLY THE SAME TONES as the relative major.

2. The MELODIC Minor Scale.

This scale uses the notes of the NATURAL MINOR, but in the ASCENDING scale, the 6th and 7th tones are raised one half step. The descending scale is the same as the NATURAL MINOR.

3. The HARMONIC Minor Scale.

This scale uses the notes of the NATURAL MINOR, but the 7th tone is raised one half step, both ascending and descending.

IMPORTANT: The sharps used to indicate the raised tones in minor scales are ACCIDENTALS. Therefore, they are not included in the key signature.

Scales should be practiced daily: (1) Both hands legato.
(2) Both hands staccato.

Spanish Dance

Moderato

Palmer-Lethco

KEY of A MINOR, RELATIVE of C MAJOR
Key Signature: NO SHARPS, NO FLATS

FOR A DIFFERENT EFFECT, PLAY THE L.H. TRIADS IN "SPANISH DANCE" AS FOLLOWS:

etc.

CIRCLE THE ROOT OF EACH L.H. TRIAD IN "SPANISH DANCE."

INTRODUCING "OVERLAPPING PEDAL"

The following sign is used to indicate **OVERLAPPING PEDAL**.

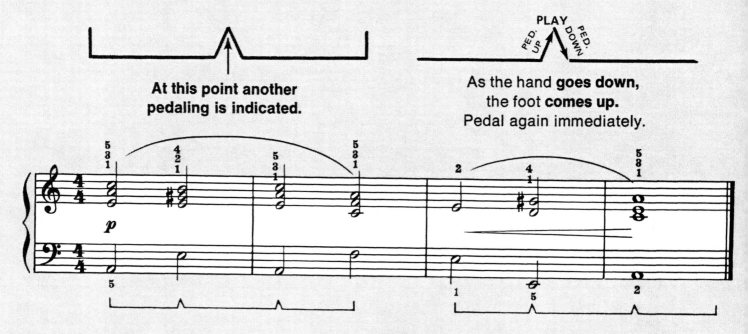

At this point another pedaling is indicated.

As the hand **goes down**, the foot **comes up**. Pedal again immediately.

Go Down, Moses

Adagio moderato

KEY of A MINOR

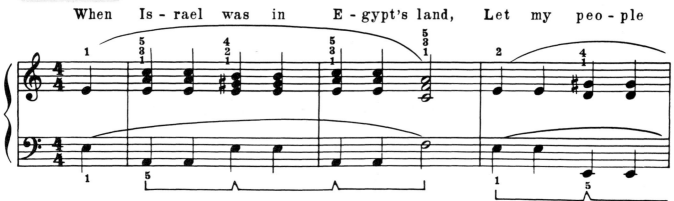

When   Is - rael   was   in   E - gypt's land,   Let   my   peo - ple

IMPORTANT: Choose your own dynamics. Write them in the music.

CIRCLE THE ROOT OF EACH R.H. TRIAD AND OF EACH L.H. TRIAD IN "GO DOWN MOSES."

WARM-UP FOR "HARVEST DANCE"

Practice with a very loose wrist. Begin slowly. Gradually increase speed.

Harvest Dance

(A POLYTONAL PIECE)

TONAL music is music in a definite key. **POLY** is a Greek term meaning "more than one." Music played in more than one key at the same time is called **POLYTONAL** music. In HARVEST DANCE the R.H. plays in C MAJOR while the L.H. plays in A MINOR.

This piece is in **BINARY,** or **TWO-PART** form.
The two parts are called **Section A** and **Section B.** This form is A B.

Allegro

Old Folk Dance

✱ ₵ This time signature is **ALLA BREVE,** sometimes called "CUT TIME."
This indicates $\frac{2}{2}$ time. Count ONE for each HALF NOTE, etc.

Section B

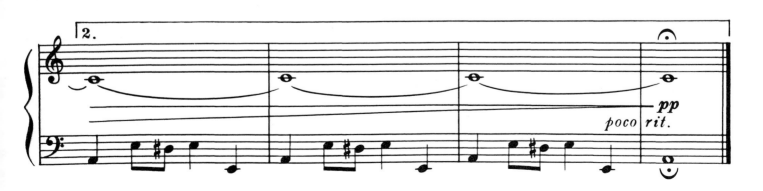

THE **D** MINOR SCALES IN CONTRARY MOTION

D minor is the relative minor of **F** major. Key signature = one flat (B♭).
Practice each scale with hands separately, then together.

1. The NATURAL Minor Scale

Same tones as the relative major.

This scale is also the AEOLIAN SCALE, transposed.

2. The MELODIC Minor Scale

ASCENDING: The 6th and 7th tones are raised one half-step.
DESCENDING: Same as the NATURAL MINOR.

3. The HARMONIC Minor Scale

ASCENDING and DESCENDING: The 7th tone is raised one half-step.

VERY IMPORTANT! Scales should be practiced daily:
        (1) Both hands legato.
        (2) Both hands staccato.

The great Italian composer and violinist, Arcangelo Corelli, lived from 1653 to 1713. He left a great treasury of instrumental compositions, most of which were written for stringed instruments and harpsichord.

Sarabanda

Andante moderato

KEY of D MINOR, RELATIVE OF F MAJOR
Key Signature: ONE FLAT (B♭)

A. Corelli

The **SARABANDA** is the Italian version of the French **SARABANDE.** This is an ancient dance, believed to have originated in the Orient. It became popular in Spain in the 1600's and later was adopted by all of Europe. By the time of Corelli it had assumed a noble and rather majestic character. It is always in three-in-a-measure time, with its phrases beginning on the first beat of the measure.

Introduction and Dance

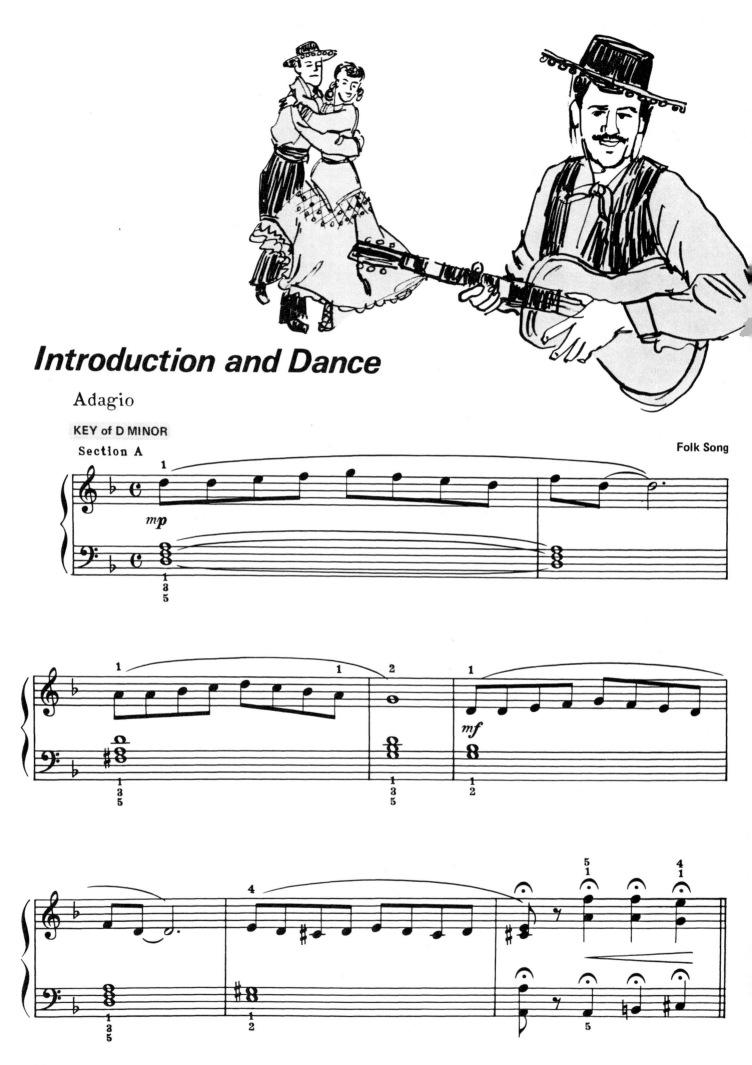

Adagio

KEY of D MINOR

Section A

Folk Song

Allegro moderato

Section B

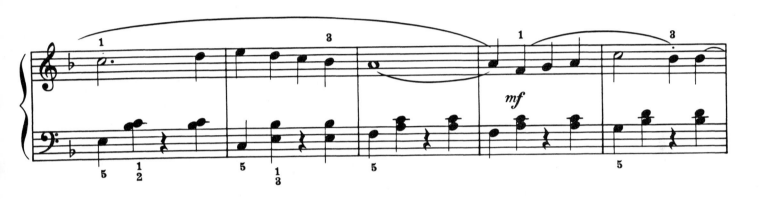

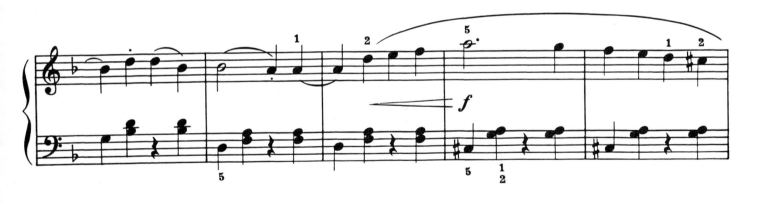

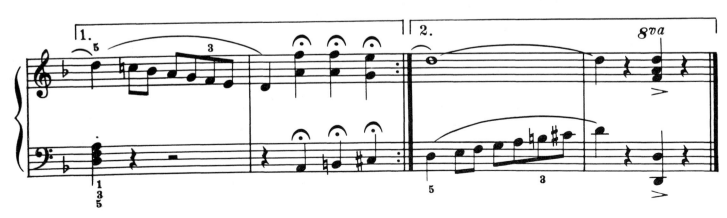

THE E MINOR SCALES IN CONTRARY MOTION

E minor is the relative minor of **G** major. Key signature = one sharp (F#).
Practice each scale with hands separately, then together.

1. The NATURAL Minor Scale

Same tones as the relative major.
This scale is also the AEOLIAN SCALE, transposed.

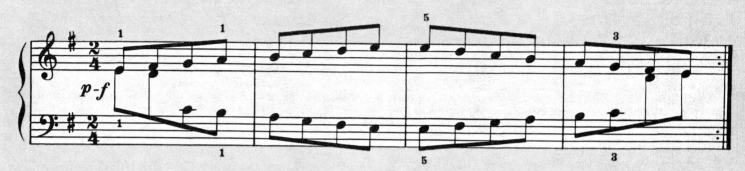

2. The MELODIC Minor Scale

ASCENDING: The 6th and 7th tones are raised one half-step.
DESCENDING: Same as the NATURAL MINOR.

3. The HARMONIC Minor Scale

ASCENDING and DESCENDING: The 7th tone is raised one half-step.

VERY IMPORTANT! Scales should be practiced daily:

    (1) Both hands legato.
    (2) Both hands staccato.

Black is the Color of My True Love's Hair

In this selection, the time signatures change from $\frac{2}{4}$ to $\frac{4}{4}$ and back several times. Simply count "one" for each quarter, "one and" for each pair of eighths, etc., throughout the piece. STEMS UP = R.H.   STEMS DOWN = L.H.

Adagio moderato *(freely)*

KEY of E MINOR, RELATIVE of G MAJOR
Key Signature: ONE SHARP (F♯)

Traditional

TRANSPOSE TO THE KEY OF **D** MINOR by moving each note down one WHOLE STEP. Observe the key signature of **D** MINOR.

PORTATO

A slur enclosing a group of notes with staccato dots above or below them indicates a touch **between** staccato and legato, called **PORTATO. Portato** is an Italian word. It means **carried.** The tone is carried a little longer than the normal length of the staccato.

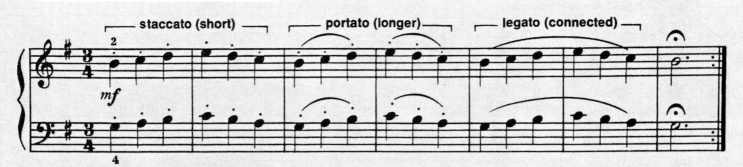

If only the **LAST** note of a slurred group has a staccato dot above or below it, it is played with a normal staccato touch, rather than **portato.** See measures 2 and 4 below:

Bagatelle

This piece is in **TERNARY,** or **THREE-PART** form. This form is A B A.

R. Köhler

A **BAGATELLE** is a short, whimsical piece.

SECTION B, in E MINOR
(Relative of G MAJOR)

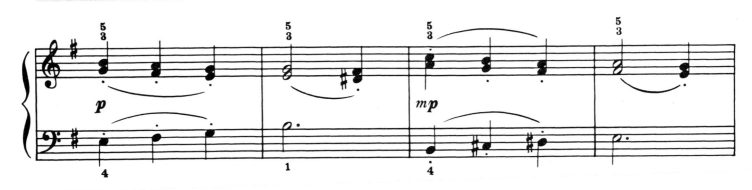

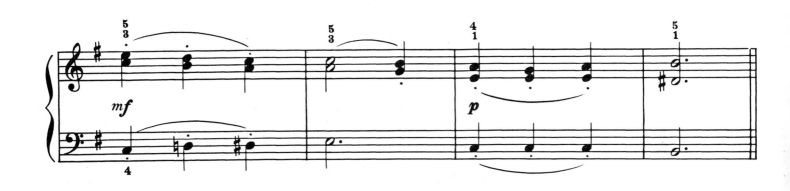

SECTION A, in G MAJOR

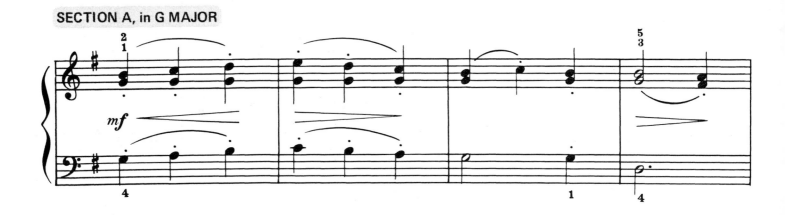

HARMONIC MINOR SCALES IN PARALLEL MOTION

IMPORTANT!!

In each of the scales on this page, the 3rd FINGERS of the R.H. and L.H. always play at the SAME TIME.

A HARMONIC MINOR (Relative of C Major)

D HARMONIC MINOR (Relative of F Major)

E HARMONIC MINOR (Relative of G Major)

NATURAL OR PURE MINOR SCALES
IN PARALLEL MOTION

These scales are exactly the same as the above, except the 7th degree of each scale is not raised. Simply play the above scales without observing the accidental sharps. DO OBSERVE all sharps or flats in the key signature.

All of the scales on this page should be practiced daily:

1. In parallel motion, legato.
2. In parallel motion, staccato.
3. In contrary motion, legato.
4. In contrary motion, staccato.

Allegretto in A Minor

(THEME FROM THE 7th SYMPHONY)

L. van Beethoven

*Allegretto

*__Allegretto__ is an Italian word meaning "rather lively." When this tempo marking is used, the music is played somewhat slower than **Allegro.**

29

The House of the Rising Sun

Moderato

Folk Song

KEY of E MINOR

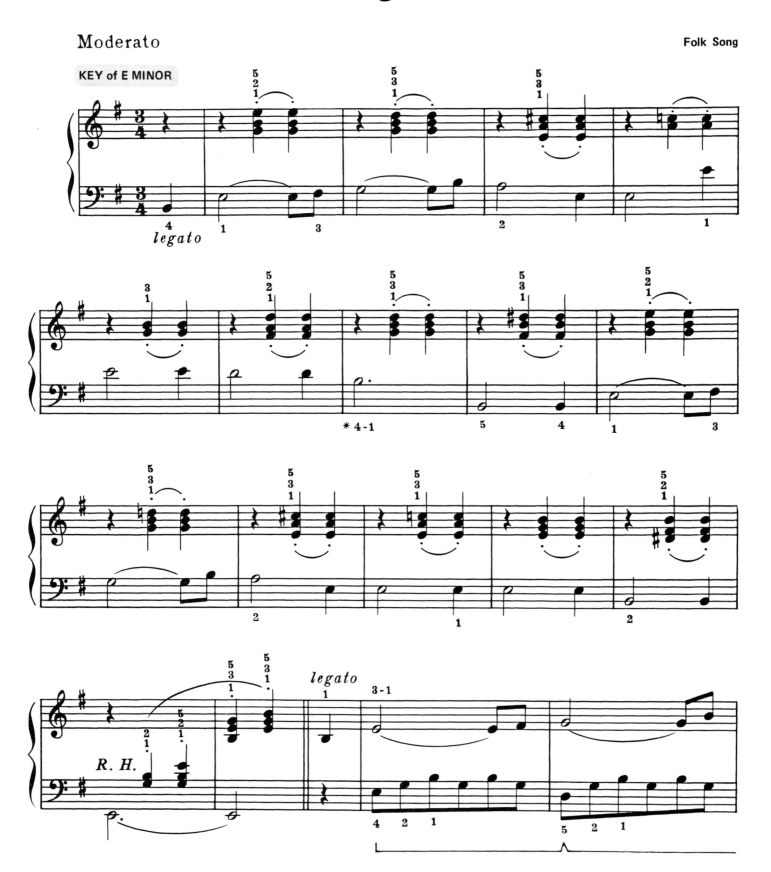

* **4-1** PLAY WITH 4, THEN SUBSTITUTE 1 WITHOUT RE-STRIKING THE KEY.

IMPORTANT: Choose your own dynamics. Write them in the music.

"DROPS AND LIFTS"

Playing these "DROPS AND LIFTS" daily will help you:

1. make more beautiful tones.
2. make more musical phrase endings.
3. increase the span between the thumb and fifth finger.
4. recognize the sound of each interval.

DROP on the 1st note and LIFT on the 2nd note of each slurred pair.
The 2nd note of each slurred pair should be a little softer than the 1st.

DROP ON THE SIDE OF THE THUMB NAIL.
LIFT FROM THE WRIST.

DROP ON THE OUTSIDE TIP OF THE 5th FINGER.   LIFT FROM THE WRIST.

IMPORTANT!! TRANSPOSE ALL THE MUSIC ON THIS PAGE:

1. To the key of G major. Begin each line on G.
2. To the key of D major. Begin each line on D.

Ballet Music from "LA GIOCONDA"

Ponchielli

TRANSPOSE THIS PIECE TO THE KEY OF C MAJOR BY PLAYING EACH NOTE ONE WHOLE STEP LOWER.

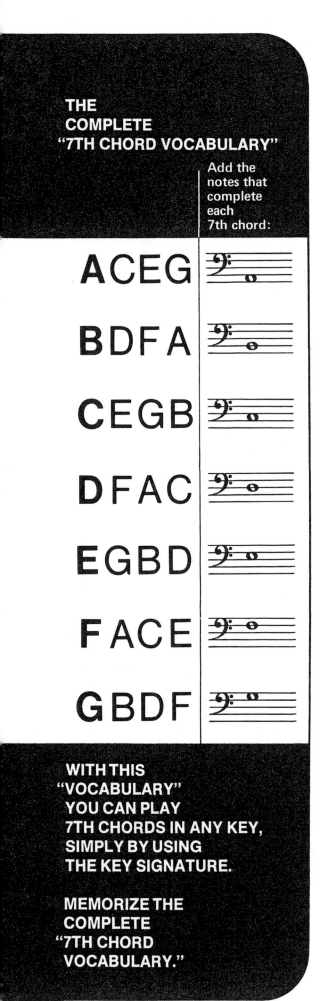

THE COMPLETE "7TH CHORD VOCABULARY"

Add the notes that complete each 7th chord:

ACEG

BDFA

CEGB

DFAC

EGBD

FACE

GBDF

WITH THIS "VOCABULARY" YOU CAN PLAY 7TH CHORDS IN ANY KEY, SIMPLY BY USING THE KEY SIGNATURE.

MEMORIZE THE COMPLETE "7TH CHORD VOCABULARY."

SEVENTH CHORDS

A **SEVENTH CHORD** MAY BE FORMED
BY ADDING TO THE **ROOT POSITION TRIAD**
A NOTE THAT IS A **SEVENTH** ABOVE THE ROOT.

THE FOUR NOTES OF A SEVENTH CHORD ARE:

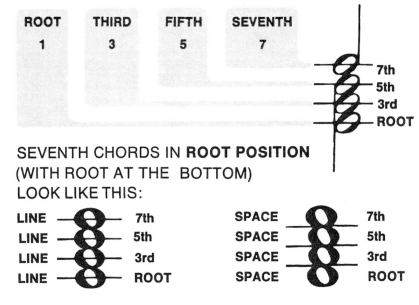

ROOT	THIRD	FIFTH	SEVENTH
1	3	5	7

SEVENTH CHORDS IN **ROOT POSITION**
(WITH ROOT AT THE BOTTOM)
LOOK LIKE THIS:

LINE — 7th	SPACE — 7th
LINE — 5th	SPACE — 5th
LINE — 3rd	SPACE — 3rd
LINE — ROOT	SPACE — ROOT

SEVENTH CHORDS MAY BE BUILT
ON ANY NOTE OF ANY SCALE.

SEVENTH CHORDS IN C MAJOR
PLAY: Stems up = R.H.   Stems down = L.H.

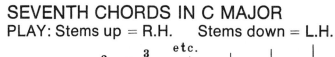

The 5th is often omitted from the 7th chord.
This makes it simple to play with one hand.
PLAY WITH L.H.

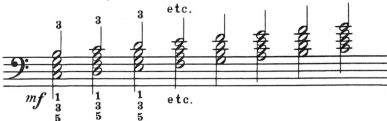

The 3rd is sometimes omitted.
PLAY WITH L.H.

PLAN FOR A TUNE USING SEVENTH CHORDS

With this plan you can make a tune using seventh chords for the left hand accompaniment.

Practice the plan until you can play it with ease.

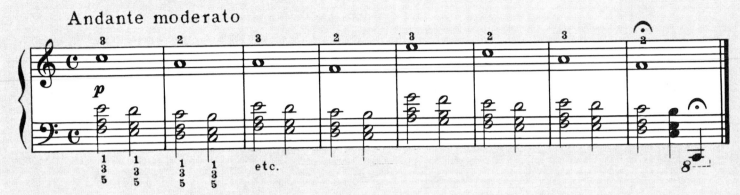

IN THIS PLAN THE MOTIVES ARE PLAYED WITH THE R.H.

Motives 1 and 2 are to be used ALTERNATELY.

MOTIVE 1 is used in the FIRST measure, starting on C. MOTIVE 2 is used in the SECOND measure, starting on A. Continue to alternate motives 1 and 2 throughout the plan. The plan shows the starting note for EACH motive.

Motives 3 and 4 are to be used ALTERNATELY.

Use MOTIVE 3 in the FIRST measure. Follow with MOTIVE 4 in the SECOND measure. Continue to alternate motives 3 and 4 throughout. Begin EACH motive on the note shown in the plan.

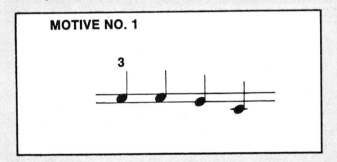

CREATE A MOTIVE OF YOUR OWN AND USE IT IN THE PLAN.

Sonatina in C Major (FIRST MOVEMENT)

The word **sonata** was first used to mean "music to be played," as opposed to **cantata,** "music to be sung." A **sonatina** is a short **sonata.** Most **sonatas** have three movements. Many **sonatinas** have only two. This sonatina has another movement, but each movement may be played as a complete selection. The form is **TERNARY,** A-B-A, plus a short CODA.

Tobias Haslinger was an Austrian music publisher. He was a close friend of Beethoven, who held him in high esteem.

Allegro non tanto

Tobias Haslinger
(1787-1842)

Non tanto, in Italian, means "not too much."
Allegro non tanto = "Not too fast."
Grazioso is an Italian word meaning "gracefully."

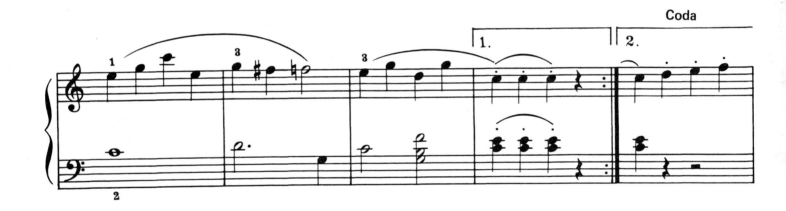

IMPORTANT! Circle the 7th chords in the Sonatina and identify the root of each one.
Which ones have the 5th omitted?   Which have the 3rd omitted?

Echo Rock

The chords in the 1st measure are: **D TRIAD in root position**
G TRIAD in 2nd inversion
D 7th CHORD with 3rd omitted
G TRIAD in 2nd inversion

ANALYZE THE CHORDS IN THE REMAINING MEASURES.

INVERSIONS OF SEVENTH CHORDS

STUDY THIS PAGE.

Seventh chords may be played in the following positions:

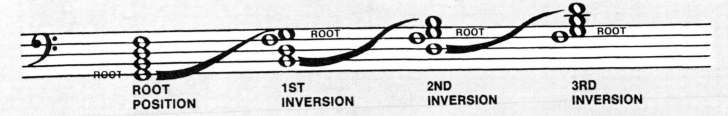

ROOT POSITION   1ST INVERSION   2ND INVERSION   3RD INVERSION

The 1st, 2nd and 3rd inversions are easily recognized by the interval of a 2nd in each chord. The TOP NOTE OF THE 2nd IS ALWAYS THE ROOT.

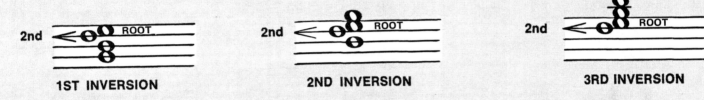

1ST INVERSION   2ND INVERSION   3RD INVERSION

Seventh chords are often played with either the 5th or the 3rd omitted.

When the 5th is omitted, there is no 2nd inversion:

ROOT POSITION   1ST INVERSION   3RD INVERSION
└── 5TH OMITTED ──┘

When the 3rd is omitted, there is no 1st inversion:

ROOT POSITION   2ND INVERSION   3RD INVERSION
└── 3RD OMITTED ──┘

PLAY THE FOLLOWING:

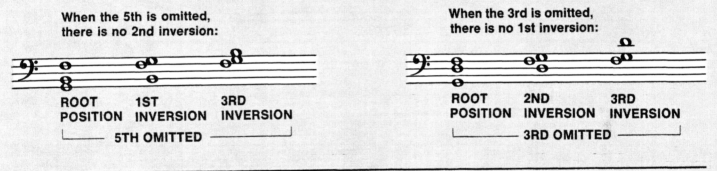

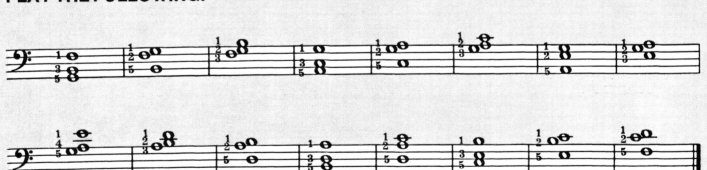

Circle the ROOT in each of the above seventh chords.
If the interval of a 2nd appears in the chord, the TOP NOTE of the 2nd is the root.
If there is no 2nd, the LOWEST NOTE is the root.

THEME FROM
The Polovetsian Dances

Play the L.H. alone until you can play it with ease. Then add the R.H.

Moderato

A. Borodin

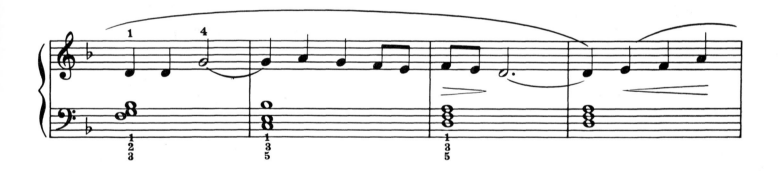

Circle the root of each triad and each 7th chord.

MELODIC MINOR SCALES

IMPORTANT!!

In each of the scales on this page, the 3rd FINGERS of the R.H. and L.H. always play at the SAME TIME.

A MELODIC MINOR (relative of C major)

D MELODIC MINOR (relative of F major)

E MELODIC MINOR (relative of G major)

You should now be practicing the following scales DAILY, in parallel and in contrary motion:

A HARMONIC MINOR . . . A NATURAL MINOR . . . A MELODIC MINOR
D HARMONIC MINOR . . . D NATURAL MINOR . . . D MELODIC MINOR
E HARMONIC MINOR . . . E NATURAL MINOR . . . E MELODIC MINOR

ALSO: C MAJOR . . . . . G MAJOR . . . . . D MAJOR

and hands separately: F MAJOR.

Always make each scale sound MUSICAL!

INTRODUCING 2-PART WRITING

Very often one hand must play two melodies at the same time.

First or principal melody:

Second or counter melody:

When both melodies are written on ONE staff, the note-stems of the UPPER melody are turned UP, and the note-stems of the LOWER melody are turned DOWN. This is called TWO-PART WRITING.

Play both melodies at the same time with the RIGHT HAND ONLY:

Listen for all the different HARMONIC INTERVALS that result as you play.
Name the harmonic intervals aloud.

Franz Peter Schubert was born January 31, 1797, in Vienna. He was a musical genius and composed his first symphony when he was only 16 years old. His incidental music to the drama **Rosamunde** includes some of his most popular melodies. **Entr'acte,** pronounced AHN-TRAHKT, is French for "between the acts." Music with this title is composed especially to be played between the acts of an opera or a play.

Franz Schubert

Entr'acte
from ROSAMUNDE

Andante moderato

Ukrainian Bell Carol

Allegro

M. Leontovich

KEY of A MINOR

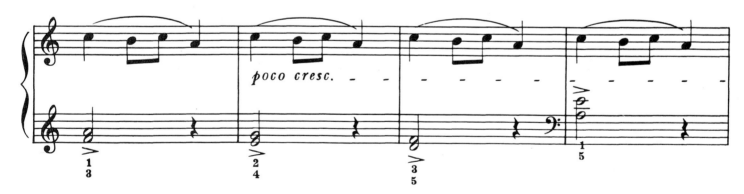

REVIEW

1. Play the following scales with hands together in parallel and contrary motion: **(25 points)**

   C MAJOR   **A** MINOR (all 3 forms)
   G MAJOR   **D** MINOR (all 3 forms)
   D MAJOR   **E** MINOR (all 3 forms)   (2 points for each scale)

   Play the **F** Major scale with hands separately. (1 point)

2. Identify and demonstrate the touch used in each of these measures: **(8 points)**
   (2 points for each measure)

3. Give the meaning of each of the following terms: **(9 points)**

8va SEGUE	POCO	GRAZIOSO
TERNARY	ALLA BREVE	ALLEGRETTO
BINARY	NON TANTO	OSTINATO

4. Write the complete 7th chord vocabulary: **(7 points)**

- -

5. Circle the root of each of the following 7th chords: **(8 points)**

6. Play 3 pieces from memory for your teacher. **(15 points)**

7. Transpose "BALLET MUSIC from LA GIOCONDA" to the key of **C** Major
   by playing each note one whole step lower. **(10 points)**

8. Match each major scale with its relative minor: **(9 points)**
   (3 points each answer)

   1. **F** MAJOR   ☐ **A** MINOR
   2. **G** MAJOR   ☐ **D** MINOR
   3. **C** MAJOR   ☐ **E** MINOR

9. Fill in the missing key signatures: **(9 points)**
   (3 points each)

   1. D MINOR   **2. E MINOR**   **3. A MINOR**

PERFECT SCORE: 100 POINTS.   **YOUR SCORE:** _____ **points.**